SKILLS
INSTRUCTION

GRAHAM FOSTER/JUDY MACKAY/CLAUDETTE MILLER

SKILLS
INSTRUCTION
IN A LANGUAGE ARTS PROGRAM

Pembroke Publishers Limited

© 1992 Pembroke Publishers Limited
538 Hood Road
Markham, Ontario
L3R 3K9

Canadian Cataloguing in Publication Data

Foster, Graham
  Skills instruction in a language arts program

Includes bibliographical references.
ISBN 0-921217-90-0

1. English language – Instruction and study
(Elementary). I. MacKay, Judy. II. Miller,
Claudette. III. Title.

LB1576.F67 1992   372.6'044   C92-094770-0

The concept for this book originated from a curriculum document produced by the Calgary Roman Catholic Separate School District No. 1. Original writing team members also included: Lindy Arndt, Elizabeth Donovan, Michelle Fry, Diane Little, Jackie Lutz, Lina Rosenburg, and Rose Ferreirinha.

Editor: Joanne Close
Design: John Zehethofer
Cover Photography: Ajay Photographics
Typesetting: Jay Tee Graphics Ltd.

This book was produced with the generous assistance of the Government of Ontario through the Ministry of Culture and Communications.

Printed and bound in Canada by Webcom Limited
9 8 7 6 5 4 3 2 1

Table of Contents

Foreword

Recent theory and research have had a dramatic impact on many beliefs about learning, teaching, language, and literacy. These developments have also altered beliefs related to the place of skills within the language program. Current thinking about skills reflects a holistic perspective toward language learning. This perspective views skills not as ends in themselves, but as part of an extensive language repertoire to be developed by each learner.

In the past, the term "skills" was used to indicate a relatively narrow band of abilities related to such elements as conventions, surface features, grammar, and mechanics. Current thinking, however, defines "skills" in much broader terms that include the development of strategies and the application of knowledge. This perspective, then, maintains that language skills are developed through meaningful use, and gives rise to a number of far-reaching implications for effective skills development in a holistic language program. These implications are the focus of this organization.

Organization

Educators constantly seek answers to questions about learning and instructional practice. With this in mind, the authors have organized around a number of broad themes questions related to holistic language programs. These themes are:

- characteristics of holistic language programs;
- standards of student achievement;
- current terminology;
- the meaning of the word, "skills";
- holistic instructional procedures.

The questions, thirty-one in all, are followed by responses that are written in a concise, straight-forward manner. Where appropriate, classroom examples have been included.

Introduction

In a holistic language program, teachers organize activities that focus on meaning. Often students will consider the ideas, emotions, responses, and experiences related to their current reading and writing. Students read and write frequently, typically selecting reading content, writing topics, and literary forms. Through meaningful language activity, students explore, develop, and apply a wide range of skills.

A holistic language learning program does not imply that teachers ignore direct skills instruction. Instead, the teacher usually chooses specific skills for direct instruction, *after* students have engaged in independent or supported reading and writing. Direct skills instruction, then, follows, rather than precedes, student work. The holistic teacher chooses those skills that should be taught directly on the basis of ongoing observations and emerging student needs.

For example, when reviewing current pieces in students' writing folders, the teacher notices that many students are having difficulty organizing ideas. Consequently, he or she teaches a mini-lesson on clustering strategies. The mini-lesson models for students how information can be grouped and organized. In another case, the teacher notices that students tend to substitute story summaries for interpretations of meaning. During subsequent lessons, he or she instructs students on how summaries can be used as a lead-in to the next step—expression of themes, emotions, and experiences.

Following the lessons, these teachers include the skill of clustering within their evaluations. As well, skills would be included when they help students engage in self-evaluation. In this way, student meaning-making and communication of meaning are at the center of direct skills instruction.

I

Skills Teaching in a Holistic Language Program

For some teachers, the idea of implementing and managing a holistic language program may cause some concerns. This section addresses some of those concerns by outlining the goals of holistic language programs, the teacher's role, the place of skills, philosophies of learning, and the meeting of local curriculum objectives.

What are the goals of a holistic language program?

The goal of any holistic language program is to consistently involve students in exploring, constructing, and communicating meaning. It is the fundamental focus on meaning that determines general goals related to skills development.

Goals within a holistic language program include:

- involving students in significant language situations that are meaningful and relevant to them;
- encouraging student ownership of language processes;
- encouraging student responsibility for personal learning and skills development;
- developing student awareness of options and strategies in all language situations;
- encouraging students to understand that expository, narrative, and poetic language may require different strategies and formats;
- developing student ability to discuss and to control language and literacy processes consciously;
- developing connecting links, not only between literary works and daily activities, but among themes, experiences, ideas, and concepts;
- using student work to diagnose and respond to emerging needs with appropriate skills instruction;
- developing skills within the broader context of an activity, theme, unit, or topic;
- developing student awareness of which skills to select and to apply at which time (transfer);

- maintaining a balance among the various aspects of language, such as fluency, content, vocabulary, organization, meaning, conventions, and presentation;
- ensuring that the language program includes opportunities for students to explore, understand, and construct skills, as well as to communicate their understanding of them.

What is the teacher's role in holistic language instruction?

Within a holistic language program, the role of the teacher is multifaceted. During the course of the year, the teacher's role may involve the following aspects.

Community Builder

The community builder creates an environment in which students feel comfortable taking risks and solving problems.

Guide

As students explore the world of language, it is important that they have a knowledgeable and accessible guide. A guide supports students in new situations, lets them in on secrets of skillful use, and stands back until needed.

Coach

A coach plays a critical role in taking learners from "where they are" and encouraging their development through demonstrating, modeling, prompting, providing ample practice time, and communicating about progress.

Director

A director organizes, energizes, and supervises the activities of the group in order to efficiently achieve program goals and to avoid chaos.

Manager

A manager communicates rules, expectations, and

procedures in order to ensure the smooth running of day-to-day classroom operations.

Problem solver

A problem solver provides a valuable model for students and encourages them in their ongoing problem-solving experiences.

Instructor

An instructor's role is to develop knowledge in a systematic manner on the basis of informed diagnosis through advice, support, examples, models, and experiences. A holistic perspective includes the important element of direct teaching within the teacher's repertoire.

Facilitator

A facilitator provides an environment for colleagues and students that fosters engagement in worthwhile activities and tasks, reflects on relevant processes, and helps to achieve goals that have been jointly set. An effective teacher–facilitator empowers students toward growth and independence.

Evaluator

An evaluator gives expert judgment based on experience, knowledge, and research. An evaluator documents progress, diagnoses needs, communicates clearly to both students and parents, and engages students in frequent self-evaluation. An evaluator gives a professional judgment based on experience, knowledge, and classroom research.

In implementing a meaning-centered language program, teachers internalize, adapt, and balance a wide range of roles in their daily practice.

Where do specific skills "fit" in a holistic program?

Language use involves the orchestration of hundreds of skills in any given task. Any language program that moves students through a skills sequence, one skill at a time, is unsuccessful. A more successful language program recognizes that students have a wide repertoire of skills under control and builds from there.

A holistic program does not preclude instruction in specific skills. However, specific skills are highlighted and receive direct instruction only when student work indicates a readiness and a need. Many skills are learned in an embedded manner as students work with language in meaningful ways.

For example, to be successful in narrative writing, students combine a range of skills, including those listed below and many others:

- establishing and resolving the story's conflict;
- developing plausible characters;
- dramatizing action (showing rather than telling);
- using specific diction;
- varying sentence patterns;
- following conventions of usage and spelling.

Each skill has related subskills, such as the rules for capitalization, punctuation, and standard usage related to conventions. It is impossible to select any of these skills or subskills for direct instruction until students have written part or all of their stories.

The holistic language teacher realizes the futility of isolated skills instruction; therefore, he or she helps students to develop skills within a meaningful context, as shown on the following diagram.

```
┌─────────────────────────────────────────┐
│   MEANING MAKING WITH WHOLE TEXT         │
└─────────────────────────────────────────┘
            ↘               ↙
┌─────────────────────────────────────────┐
│   Choosing an element to examine more     │
│   closely on the basis of student need,   │
│        interests, or strengths            │
│                                           │
│    Deciding features, rules, criteria     │
└─────────────────────────────────────────┘
            ↖               ↗
┌─────────────────────────────────────────┐
│  APPLYING WHAT YOU HAVE LEARNED           │
│  TO MEANING MAKING WITH                   │
│  ANOTHER WHOLE TEXT                       │
└─────────────────────────────────────────┘
```

How does this current perspective on skills development differ from the view that was held in the past?

The major goal of holistic language programs is that students will demonstrate increasing confidence and competence in their abilities to use language to explore, construct, and communicate meaning. This is the pivotal difference between former and current perspectives on skill development. In a holistic program, the learning of a skill through opportunities for application is crucial. Students learn by engaging in reading and writing activities; there is *no* other way.

An excellent example of this principle is provided by one student's rather humorous story about the school swimming program. Limited access to the local pool meant that the swimming unit began somewhat ahead of the available pool time. An enterprising teacher made use of the time by involving the students in extensive stroke-improvement lessons while students lay on benches in the gym. All students, swimmers and nonswimmers alike, *apparently* improved their swimming ability over the course of the unit.

Unfortunately, when the class actually entered the water sometime later, the results were somewhat less spectacular. The students had not been engaged in a "genuine" task, but had focused on isolated skills development; subsequently they experienced considerable difficulty with transfer. The teacher's time would have been better spent coaching, teaching, and modeling on the basis of the students' needs as they worked within the context of the water.

This basic principle may be applied to every learning situation, including the development and eventual control of language literacy skills. Within the classroom, the context for the learner is authentic communication through language. Skills instruction should *never* be divorced from meaningful applications.

How can a holistic program be related to a local curriculum mandate?

A local curriculum mandate usually lists skills and concepts students are expected to learn. In deciding what to highlight from the mandated list, the holistic language teacher:

- observes students as they work with complete text;
- analyzes student work for area of strength and need;
- selects skills appropriate for direct instruction and those appropriate for embedding;
- encourages student goal-setting related to individual need;
- celebrates improvements and successes in achievement.

II

Standards

The holistic perspective on skills has implications for both student evaluation and teacher standards. This section attempts to clarify some of the questions that teachers often raise about standards and expectations.

What expectations should students have at the beginning of each grade?

No matter what the grade level, teachers can expect that the students they receive at the beginning of the year will have a wide range of abilities. Grade levels do not capture the students' abilities, needs, or interests, and must never be employed as the sole indicator of "appropriate" choice of skills and content to be taught in the upcoming year.

Students come to school from a wide range of backgrounds and experiences and have varying capabilities. Generally, teachers need to accept these differences; there is no alternative. At the same time, effective planning balances specific student needs, interests, and abilities with the mandated program.

Teacher expectations for student performance should always be related to the major goal of developing effective, independent readers and writers. Within a holistic program, the focus of evaluation is on documenting the growth of each child in terms of both product and process. Over the course of the year, it is expected that all students will move along a developmental continuum toward increased control of language processes. Many teachers committed to holistic instruction have been able to document dramatic growth in their students' language abilities.

How can such a broad range of student abilities be assessed by one teacher?

Informal, ongoing, diagnostic evaluation is the key to effective assessment of the broad range of student abilities.

As teachers work with their students, they use many informal methods to assess current language capabilities. These assessments take the form of observations, group marking sessions with colleagues, interviews, anecdotal comments, checklists, analysis of work samples, portfolios, and a range of evaluation techniques detailed in current professional literature.

Initial assessment provides benchmarks of the students' current capabilities and also serves to identify students who require additional, in-depth diagnosis. Many teachers committed to holistic instruction keep samples and records of their students' yearly work in order to document progress over time. These initial benchmarks are also valuable when students have the opportunity to:

- reflect on initial work and set personal goals;
- apply pre-determined criteria to their own work;
- compare work samples in order to note progress.

Additional management strategies related to meeting the range of needs are included in Section V of this document.

How can teachers deal with the wide variety of standards for skills that may exist between classrooms?

The best way for teachers to gain a sense of appropriate standards is to implement a program based on the mandated program, current professional literature, and their own professional judgment. When teachers participate in group marking and discuss criteria, objectives, and evaluation procedures, they enhance their professional judgments and develop specific standards. If opportunities for group marking do not present themselves at the school level, consultation with colleagues who teach at the same grade level can be equally helpful.

Teachers may also consult the core resources authorized for their grade level as indicative of the type of material students should be able to manage with instructional assistance.

III

Current Terminology

In any profession, it is easy to fall into comfortable jargon. In education today, new phrases and terms reflect the current perspective of literacy and language learning. Unfortunately, common usage does not ensure common interpretation. This section is intended to clarify some of the current jargon used by educators in relation to skill development.

What does the phrase "moving from whole to part to whole" mean and how can it be accomplished?

Current educational theory states that reading and writing are meaning-building processes. The phrase, "moving from whole to part to whole", reminds teachers of the need to present students with whole meaningful selections before asking them to work with smaller parts. Within this context, teachers can focus on appropriate skills areas such as details, story structure, paragraphing, dialogue, or descriptive language according to student need.

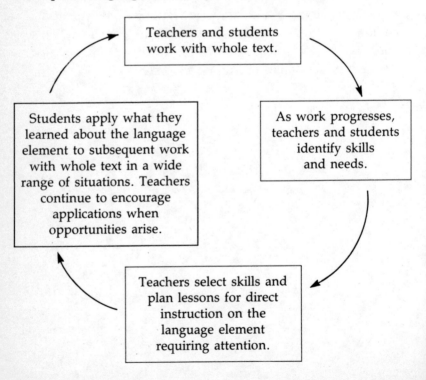

Teachers and students work with whole text.

As work progresses, teachers and students identify skills and needs.

Teachers select skills and plan lessons for direct instruction on the language element requiring attention.

Students apply what they learned about the language element to subsequent work with whole text in a wide range of situations. Teachers continue to encourage applications when opportunities arise.

For example, in their reading of poems, students demonstrate difficulty in understanding imagery and in relating imagery to an author's meaning. In subsequent lessons, the teacher reviews imagery, models how readers link imagery and meaning, reviews imagery in other media, such as film, and encourages students to find and revise examples of imagery in their own writing.

Finally, the teacher asks students to transfer and apply their knowledge of the imagery whenever they read other poems.

What does "teaching in context" mean?

When teachers talk about context, they are typically referring to the larger environment or background in which learning occurs. Teaching in context, then, centers on encouraging students to fit in their new learning with what they know already. In this way, a learner is able to link new knowledge with that that is known—a starting point for the absorption and processing of new knowledge.

As teachers make instructional decisions, they consider each of the contexts—self, instructional sequence, school environment, and society.

Teaching in context means that teachers:

- help students access previous related experience and knowledge;
- build background knowledge with students;
- immerse students in many related literary texts;
- encourage students to link a language technique with the writer's purpose and meaning;
- allow students to formulate questions they want answered about what they are reading and writing;
- invite students to articulate their own meanings and responses;
- engage in a wide range of tasks related to the topic or focus of the unit;
- select appropriate skills based on student work with complete texts and authentic language tasks.

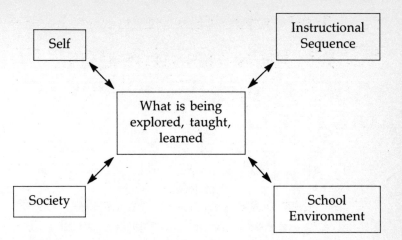

The context of "self" means the individual student's prior knowledge, interests, and rates of learning. The context of "instructional sequence" means there is a consistent concern, by both the teacher and the learner, about how a particular skill, fact, or concept fits into what is already known and what will be learned in subsequent lessons. The context of "school environment" means that unique characteristics of each school are kept in mind. The context of society means that what is learned is linked to current events and broader world knowledge.

Teaching in context is a variation of the theme that instructional parts must always be related to meaningful wholes. The learners must always understand how what they are doing fits into the larger picture.

When is "direct teaching" appropriate in a holistic program?

In a holistic language program, direct teaching occurs when the teacher recognizes the need to address a specific skill as students explore, construct, and communicate meaning. Effective direct instruction usually involves small groups or individuals rather than the whole class. Small groups should be flexible, changing as students' needs of skills and contexts evolve.

To illustrate, students in a class will vary in their ability to be precise and colorful in diction. The teacher may decide to instruct a group of students on precise and lively diction while other students continue to work on a variety of activities. Much of the direct instruction for individuals will occur in conferences discussed in detail on pages 60-61.

What is "modeling" and when does it come into play in a holistic program?

Current professional literature frequently sounds the advice that teachers should "let students in on the secrets." The expression underlines the importance of modeling. Just as effective coaches describe and model strategies for players, so too should teachers describe and model strategies for students.

Modeling is a form of direct teaching. When modeling, the teacher does not simply describe steps or processes but attempts to *think out loud* while working with language to complete a task or activity. Modeling often involves a running commentary that occurs as the teacher works through the activity or task. For instance, research clearly indicates that effective readers predict and confirm as they read. To encourage the practice, teachers talk through their own prediction and confirmation, and sometimes remind students of the teacher's modeling.

During initial modeling sessions, the teacher demonstrates the application of a skill such as skimming, predicting, or revising while the students observe. In subsequent lessons, the teacher guides students toward independent success. Gradually, less support is necessary as the students become more independent thinkers.

Once identified needs have been addressed and related strategies modeled and taught, students require practice to make these skills and strategies their own. It becomes the teacher's responsibility to provide students with the opportunity and time to practise. Since the need for skill development surfaces in context, it is most beneficial if practice also occurs in context in order that transfer be facilitated.

IV

Types of Skills

The term "skill" has many different meanings. This section attempts to define skill from the perspective of a holistic curriculum. In addition, the section explores different types of skills and issues related to skills development.

What does the term "skill" mean?

A skill is the ability to perform a task effectively. The following diagram illustrates a balanced approach to skills development and instruction; the diagram highlights that skills work must always be related to meaning-making activities.

PROCESS SKILLS
strategies and procedures
related to how to make
meaning

MEANING MAKING

THINKING SKILLS
internal mental
operations

TRADITIONAL SKILLS
knowledge of specific
language components
and literary elements

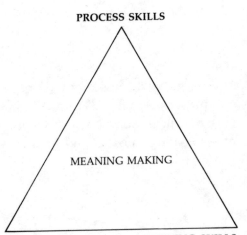

The separation of skills into these categories is not intended to suggest that these skills occur in isolation. All three types of skills are invariably embedded in and required for language tasks, and are applicable across all curriculum areas. However, it is helpful to consider all three to ensure a balanced language program.

Must learners develop their "skills" before they can read and write?

No, skills *do not* precede application. As shown by illustrations throughout this book, language learning occurs in meaningful contexts. For example, an extensive vocabulary is more effectively developed through reading and writing widely than through isolated vocabulary worksheets and memorization. In the previous example about paragraphing, students began by writing lengthy texts focused on meaning. They then considered how to organize their writing through paragraphing. Subsequent lessons might focus on improving communication at a sentence level. This sequence from whole text to specific elements is *never* reversed. Initial work always focuses on meaning and complete text.

What are "process skills" and how do teachers encourage them?

Process skills are strategies and procedures related to meaning making. Commonly recognized process skills include:

- building and activating background knowledge;
- predicting and confirming;
- checking references or re-reading when something does not make sense;
- summarizing;
- visualizing;
- recalling personal experiences related to the text;
- reviewing text so that all details are consistent with one's interpreted meaning;
- questioning to confirm or to locate additional information;
- skimming;
- locating sources of information;
- jotting notes;
- sketching;
- dramatizing;
- freewriting;
- brainstorming;
- notemaking;
- chunking and classifying;
- reviewing writing variables (role, purpose, audience, format);
- webbing ideas;
- conferring and rehearsing;
- drafting on every second line;
- leaving a space when the word doesn't come;

- beginning to write with the section that is most comfortable to the writer;
- reading aloud work to a partner;
- applying criteria to revise writing;
- publishing or presenting writing to an interested audience;
- using a known word to spell a new word;
- noting prominent details in an image.

Although this list is lengthy, it is not exhaustive. Teachers should look for additional lists of process skills within local curriculum documents.

Process skills should always be taught as a matter of repertoire so that students discover those strategies that work best for them. They should *never* be taught as a lockstep formula. Learners never stop adding to their repertoire of strategies and procedures.

Process skills are particularly important for learners who have difficulty with reading and writing. Competent readers and writers often employ process skills without conscious thought. Unfortunately, learners who are experiencing difficulty do not intuitively apply process skills or even realize that they exist. Therefore, direct teaching and modeling of process skills is particularly critical for students at risk.

As with all skills, process skills are best instructed when the need arises. For example, a teacher may work with a student who has difficulty interpreting the meaning of a poem. As they work, the teacher notices that the student expects meaning in each line of the poem. He or she suggests the strategy of noting larger chunks—perhaps indicated by punctuation and stanza breaks—and how the student can visualize these larger chunks and sketch them. The teacher also suggests that the student confer with a peer who uses these strategies successfully. Finally, the teacher challenges the student to use all these strategies with new material. In this way, the process skills of chunking, visualizing, and sketching empower the student in meaning making.

What are "thinking skills" and how do teachers encourage them?

Thinking skills are internal mental operations a learner uses in response to the demands of a language task. Various taxonomies of specific thinking skills exist and typically include categories such as:

- recalling information;
- knowing relevant facts;
- analyzing information from a variety of sources;
- synthesizing several perspectives;
- evaluating alternatives.

Within the course of completing any single language task, a learner may employ several of these mental operations at various times or at the same time. It is important for teachers to remember that thinking skills are not applied in a linear fashion, and that their presence close to the beginning or end of a particular list is not an indicator that one is better than another.

Familiarity with a broad range of thinking skills should be encouraged for *all* learners as they expand and refine their repertoire of skills and strategies through language use. Teachers can encourage the development of students' abilities with various thinking skills through modeling and direct teaching as students work to complete meaningful language tasks. From a holistic perspective, thinking skills do not occur and should *not* be taught separately from language activities and situations.

Like process skills, thinking skills are developed in context and according to student need. For example, as students analyze and evaluate a story, the teacher asks them to decide whether the protagonist in the story is justified in lying to his friend. During the discussion, the teacher encourages them:

- to state their judgment clearly;
- to employ specific evidence from the text; and
- to employ examples from personal experience that, when combined with evidence from the text, support the judgment.

If the teacher notices that students rely solely on personal experience and are careless in their textual references, he or she can move them toward more thorough evaluative thinking. If students' evidence does not support the stated judgment, then he or she will encourage them to revise their statements to achieve consistency with the evidence.

If the students continue to have difficulty in these areas, the teacher plans direct instruction on how they can apply the thinking skills of analysis and evaluation.

What are "traditional skills" and how do teachers encourage them?

Currently, when the term "traditional skill" is used, it often refers to language components and literary elements. Commonly recognized traditional skills include:

- literary elements
  — describing conflict;
  — identifying imagery;
  — recognizing plot.

- structural analysis
  — using root words to determine meaning;
  — understand meanings of prefixes and suffixes.

- grammar usage
  — avoiding sentence fragments;
  — maintaining subject-verb agreement.

- phonics
  — understanding knowledge of sound-symbol relationships such as blends or other common patterns;
  — using phonic exceptions such as *knife*.

- writing
  — organizing thoughts in paragraphs;
  — using words precisely.

- spelling
  — applying spelling patterns such as "i" before "e";
  — doubling consonants before adding an ending.

- punctuation and capitalization
  — setting up a list;
  — capitalizing proper nouns;
  — punctuating a letter;
  — using apostrophes.

These skills are important to meaning making and communicating meaning. However, traditional skill development must always occur within complete, meaningful language tasks. This means that teachers have a responsibility to consider why skills are taught and how their instruction will facilitate skills development. For example, if students are engaged in reading or writing texts that involve conversation, their need would dictate instruction in the appropriate use of quotation marks and the conventions of dialogue. Other aspects of text, identified by the teacher as a result of perusal of student work or interaction during class, would provide material for subsequent mini-lessons and/or conferences with the student.

In another instance, the teacher notices that many children spell "said" incorrectly. In a subsequent lesson, he or she discusses the word and how it is an exception to the rule. Then, the teacher adds the word to the permanent display on the bulletin board of challenge words and encourages the students to check the board when they use "said" in their writing. Once the students spell the word correctly, the teacher removes it from the list.

In a final example, a student presents a lengthy piece of writing in which all of the sentences are contained in one paragraph. The teacher recognizes a marvellous opportunity to teach organization—a traditional writing skill. The teacher then works with the student to mark chunks of meaning and to check that each chunk is focused and clear. In the days that follow, he or she takes advantage of other opportunities to work with students' writing to teach organization.

Why does it seem that the skills students have under control at one point "fall apart" when they are trying to gain control of something new or are working on a new unit?

The problem of skills temporarily "falling apart" is a function of attention or focus. As the student focuses on acquiring a new skill, so much attention is required that previously learned skills may appear to fade. This means that attention is focused on the problem at hand and retrieval of other skills is delayed. However, as the newly learned skill becomes part of the student's growing repertoire, balance returns and skills formerly under control once again receive equal attention. This process towards automaticity may be considered the final level in skill acquisition. Internalization of any new skill, strategy, or technique requires time. Teachers must be patient and persistent.

How can teachers encourage the transfer of skills?

Skills taught in one subject area are not automatically transferred to other activities or subjects that require similar skills. Teachers must strive continually through direct instruction, modeling, discussion, and comments to help students develop links between various lessons and experiences.

Teachers should provide direct teaching and modeling of the strategies across subject areas. For example, students in a science class are sometimes required to read directions for carrying out an experiment. The teacher directly teaches and models the thinking processes and strategies involved in reading directions, letting students know why they need the skill and how it helps them to carry out the experiment. The teacher makes connections to this lesson in subsequent lessons in other contexts. Communication with colleagues about development of skills in other subject areas to facilitate student awareness of links across the curriculum is also critical. This type of communication might involve interaction between colleagues working with the same class in different subjects, or between colleagues when the students move on.

Does a holistic perspective on skills mean that teachers have to change everything that they do?

No! The current view of skills is a question of evolution and refinement, not revolution. Just as teachers expect their students to grow, so too must teachers allow themselves to develop new outlooks and techniques. Provision of an effective educational program is an ongoing process that involves continuous discovery, assimilation, and refinement based on current research and professional knowledge. Many teachers have initiated a holistic language program "one risk at a time". Professional reading, sharing with colleagues, and attending conferences are critical in supporting teachers' efforts to improve their programs.

Why is it recommended that skills not be taught until students need them?

This recommendation is based on the well-documented concept that skills instruction is most meaningful when it is initiated in response to a need that arises in context. Students are able to learn skills more readily when they can see clearly why and how the learning will help them to improve language competency. Skills taught in isolation, when the students don't need or understand them, are seldom understood, applied, or transferred.

What does a diagnostic approach to skills instruction entail?

A diagnostic approach to skills instruction entails a cyclical process of evaluation that involves the following components:

- assessment of student needs, strengths, interests, weaknesses, and strategies based on teacher observations;
- observations, student work samples, portfolios, projects, etc.;
- selection of priorities for instruction (class, small group, individual);
- selection of appropriate instructional strategies (as simple as continuing to embed comments within class discussions or as direct as mini-lessons);
- implementation of appropriate instructional strategies;
- ongoing assessment to determine progress, impact of instruction, emerging needs, etc.

This view of instruction is based on the need to personalize the curriculum to address efficiently the specific abilities, interests, and needs of the particular students with whom a teacher is currently working.

Can the teaching of skills be enjoyable?

Yes! Skills instruction within the overall context of the classroom can be very enjoyable. This is particularly true when the learners' increasing control of language processes, strategies, procedures, and skills allows them to respond effectively to a wide range of language tasks. Throughout the year, students gain immense satisfaction from noting personal progress in their learning logs, personal journals, or writing folders. The learner's enthusiasm and commitment, which often accompany success, growth, and control, energize and encourage their efforts and reward teachers immensely.

What role should prescribed resources play in a holistic language program?

Resources should continue to be used as a vehicle to help teachers plan and implement programs to meet the needs of their students. In a holistic program, teachers strive to provide real language experiences with a variety of available resources. These should include students' personal background and experiences, community resources, student-produced materials, and children's literature. Resources are used to support rather than dictate the direction and content of the program.

Since skill levels vary widely within a classroom, how does the teacher manage?

When students share responsibility for learning, teachers have fewer management concerns. This means that the teacher and the students explore such options as:

- small-group methodology;
- peer teaching;
- problem-solving strategies;
- student-kept records and learning logs;
- reading and writing workshop procedures.

The critical feature of all these techniques is the high degree of student involvement they allow and encourage. Management is enhanced through record-keeping techniques such as:

- individual conference records;
- observational notes;
- writing and reading folders;
- learning logs;
- process evaluation forms and profiles that encourage student reflection;
- frequent self- and group evaluation by students;
- ongoing teacher evaluation of the program through methods such as checklists.

V

Instructional Procedures

In considering any educational question, teachers always face the difficulty of translating general recommendations and theories into specific classroom practice. This section highlights specific strategies teachers have found useful in planning and implementing instructional programs consistent with a holistic perspective.

How do teachers plan for a holistic language program?

Planning for a holistic language program is basically the same as planning for any effective instructional program. Using the local curricula and available resources, teachers develop both long- and short-range plans during the year.

Long-range plans include possible units, general objectives, core resources, a range of evaluation techniques, and a flexible time-line. The focus in long-range plans is on developing a *vision* for the year, rather than on specific concepts and skills.

Short-range plans include specific objectives that arise as a result of ongoing observation, diagnosis, and evaluation. Short-range plans elaborate specific themes, units, or topics chosen to meet the varying needs, interests, and abilities of students, as well as to achieve the objectives of local curriculum documents. They include an elaboration of:

- a major focus;
- an appropriate time-line;
- a list of materials selected from available resources;
- a possible sequence of activities;
- methods of instruction;
- specific evaluation procedures related to instructional focus and projects in the unit.

Short-range plans *must* be more than a collection of poems, stories, vocabulary lists, and activity sheets on a theme or unit. Each part of the short-range plan should be purposefully linked to the overall theme and to other parts of the unit. In all themes or units, teachers should stress strategies that help students to make meaning and apply language processes consciously.

Assessment information collected early in the year assists teachers in subsequent selection of specific instructional priorities in initial short-range plans. Throughout the year, teachers use the strengths, skills, interests, and needs of the students to determine which skills, processes, and concepts are taught and when. These considerations should also influence selection of materials.

How do teachers decide which skills are important and which are secondary?

Local curriculum documents outline the program's strategies and skills. While the goal is that students master the concepts, skills, and strategies prescribed, teachers must remain sensitive to student differences that will temper actual strategy, concept, and skills instruction. Meaning, fluency, and understanding provide the initial instructional focus, with a gradual shift to more specific language elements. Teachers select instructional priorities as they observe, diagnose, and confer with students. The initial focus for concept and skills instruction should *always* be on meaning, fluency, and understanding, with a gradual shift to more specific aspects of language as the students gain control.

Needs and interests identified for the majority of the students can be addressed initially in whole-class lessons. Additional instruction can be provided for those students who continue to experience difficulty through individual and/or small-group conferences and lessons. The teacher's repertoire of instructional procedures includes:

- whole-class lessons that address needs and interests of the majority of the students;
- individual and/or small-group conferences and lessons for students who continue to experience difficulty;
- individual and/or small-group conferences and lessons for students who are ready for extension and challenge.

When teachers consciously choose, directly teach, and emphasize skills that are appropriate for their students, plans must change from unit to unit and from year to year.

Where do workbooks, worksheets, and other skills-related materials fit in a holistic program?

As with *all* instructional materials, workbooks and worksheets should be selected carefully on the basis of individual student need and current program objectives. Worksheets are rarely appropriate when related to subskills (blends, sequence, dictionary) in whole-class instruction. More appropriate is the use of workbook pages that incorporate thinking skills, respect complete text, provide opportunities to apply strategies, and allow open-ended response. For example, workbook pages that involve cloze sheets, listing main events, thought webs, time-lines, and visual translation of text have more general applicability. However, teachers do not need to purchase workbooks to engage students in these activities.

How can teachers effectively manage their classrooms to accommodate the wide range of students' needs and abilities?

The individual and personal nature of language and learning makes the range of student need and ability inevitable. The first step in accommodating the range is to accept it as a natural event. This means that the teacher must adapt instructional methods. Many teachers use the following management techniques.

Management Technique	Example
• consciously share learning and management responsibilities with students	— students distribute and pick up materials; — students sign up for conferences when they are ready; — students select topics and projects related to the current unit; — students keep lists of problems and elements under control; — teachers expect students to monitor themselves for meaning as they read, write, listen, speak, and view;

— teachers encourage students to develop strategies to use when meaning is lost or unclear.

• vary the ways that students demonstrate abilities

— students and teachers negotiate response formats such as visual representations, oral interpretations, forms of writing;
— students engage in both individual and group projects.

• review and evaluate student work on a selective basis

— teachers identify two or three students for close observation each day;
— teachers review one or two portfolios each day;
— teachers evaluate for specific rather than global features;
— students select their best work for summative evaluation.

• establish procedures and routines so that students can function independently

— teachers train students not to interrupt student-teacher conferences;
— students know where to find what they need (e.g., pencils, dictionaries);
— teachers celebrate effective independent decision making and problem solving by students.

- build predictable activities and procedures into the timetable

  — teachers assign specific times for regular activities such as freereading, conferences, and small-group lessons;
  — teachers set aside class time to be free for observation.

- engage students in evaluation

  — teachers allow class time for presentation of projects while the teacher and other students evaluate and provide feedback;
  — students work with the teacher to determine appropriate criteria that they apply;
  — students set their own goals and reflect on their own achievement.

How can teachers evaluate student processes, strategies, and skills in a holistic program?

In planning evaluation, teachers follow four guiding principles.

1. Evaluation techniques are varied.
2. The major purpose of evaluation is to enhance learning.
3. Involvement of students in evaluation of their own work and that of others is essential.
4. Evaluation influences planning and decisions about instructions.

Some specific techniques that respect these guidelines are detailed here.

Portfolios

Portfolios are collections of dated work carefully selected by students and teachers to demonstrate the student's best work. Teachers and students negotiate the content of portfolios, as well as criteria for selection. Portfolios may contain:

• lists of books read;
• best response journal entry;
• lists of written pieces;
• best pieces of writing;
• personalized lists of skills under control and in need of attention;
• student-kept notes about goals reached;

- selected conference summaries;
- personal interest inventories and topic lists;
- checklists of forms, formats, purposes, and audiences that have been explored.

Regardless of specific contents in portfolios, students provide a written rationale for their choices.

Observation

Observation is a valuable source for monitoring development of students. In order to capitalize on the power of observation as an evaluative technique, teachers must ensure that they set aside time during the day to observe. Prior to observing, teachers should identify specifically those students, objectives, and/or activities that are to be evaluated. Formalization of the observations in notes and record sheets is important. Observation can be effectively managed if a rotational schedule is developed by the teacher.

Checklists

Checklists provide a focus for teacher observations. They are particularly helpful when developed by the teacher to reflect specific objectives and needs within each classroom. When teachers share personally developed checklists with colleagues, they:

- identify what they value in language learning;
- compare what they value with what others value;
- broaden or focus their perspective on those skills that are important in given tasks.

Interviews and Conferences

Interviews and conferences allow teachers to:

- evaluate student processes and products;

- confirm, validate, and extend impressions gained through observation;
- determine student awareness of strategies, decisions, and choices;
- make decisions about direct instruction;
- track student progress over time.

Performance Evaluation Scales

Performance evaluation scales highlight elements to be applied in assessment and specify criteria that demand teacher judgment. Some examples include:

- analytic/holistic scales for assessment of writing;
- assessment forms for oral interpretation of literature;
- criteria to assess audio/visual presentations.

Pre-specified Response

Pre-specified response includes a wide range of assessments in which students are expected to approximate a pre-determined answer. Examples of pre-specified response assessments include cloze tests, short-answer tests, retelling activities, and miscue analysis. A holistic perspective balances pre-specified response with several other forms of evaluation; it encourages students to respond in their own terms, and to gather their own evidence to support their interpretation.

How do teachers begin to implement a program that reflects a holistic view of skills development?

When they plan, all educators consider goals and objectives, learning activities, instructional resources (print, nonprint, human), and evaluation. When they decide to implement a holistic program, educators begin by considering how each of these components can be dealt with in a way that is meaningful to the current group of students. The first step is to realize that there are likely several holistic aspects already in place in the program. It is important to identify these aspects, to build upon them within the context of the students' needs, and to move in accordance with the comfort levels of everyone in the classroom.

A final word

As teachers work to implement a program that incorporates skills holistically, they can rely on several sources of support, advice, and information. These include an extensive body of professional knowledge, interactions with colleagues, support from parents and students, and reflection on their own professional experiences.

Professional sources often present a range of concise and current insights. Domestic and international organizations offer conferences, books, publications, videotapes, and guest speakers. Professionals rely on these sources for information, confirmation, extension, and challenges.

Interaction with colleagues also enhances holistic instruction. Holistic language teachers view themselves as learners. Like other learners, they thrive on the opportunity to ask questions, to investigate, to learn from others, and to celebrate successes. The practical challenges of holistic practice demand that teachers have the opportunity to discuss all aspects of their professional work—children's literature, instructional techniques, student work samples, program coordination, and communication with parents.

When teachers make direct efforts to inform and involve parents, they are rewarded with a wealth of support and celebration that enhances learning. Parents usually respond positively to information nights, volunteer programs, student-conducted tours, publication of student work, sharing of student work samples, and educational literature intended for parents. Teachers reap additional support when they make it obvious to parents what students have learned.

For holistic language teachers, the most convincing support comes from the enthusiasm, interest, and achievement of their students. Such is the teacher's greatest affirmation.

In considering the complex questions and issues that surround the topic of skills development, teachers can be assured that research and professional literature offer specific and helpful guidance. Teachers need not be isolated in grappling with the practical questions that arise daily in their classrooms. When teachers work together, they become more confident, effective professionals.

6788